MEOWTER
SPACE
ARE CATS
REALLY ALIENS?

Written by
DONALD LEMKE

Illustrated by

T0364060

RP Minis®
Hachette Book Group
1290 Avenue of the Americas, New York, NY 10104
www.runningpress.com
@Running_Press

First Edition: September 2024

Published by RP Minis, an imprint of Hachette Book Group, Inc. The RP Minis name and logo is a registered trademark of Hachette Book Group, Inc.

Running Press books may be purchased in bulk for business, educational, or promotional use. For more information, please contact your local bookseller or the Hachette Book Group Special Markets Department at Special.Markets@hbgusa.com.

The publisher is not responsible for websites (or their content) that are not owned by the publisher.

Design by Mary Boyer

ISBN: 978-0-7624-8782-0

GREETINGS EARTHLINGS

(I.E., *NOT* CATS),

By now, we all know that aliens are real, right? I mean, the United States government even confirmed it during a historic congressional hearing on Unidentified Aerial Phenomena. Per usual, this was a giant waste of time because the answers to "Is there life out there?" and "Are they already among us?" were right in front of

our faces the whole time. Actually, *on* our faces. At night. Just after we've fallen asleep.

That's right. The answers are yes and yes . . . and CATS!

Yep, the so-called "aliens" have been here all along in the form of our four-legged companions. Alley cats? Aliens. House cats? Aliens. Aristocats? Cartoon aliens. And this is, by no means, a modern phenomenon. Thousands of years ago, ancient Egyptians revered cats, worshipping them as divine spirits, and those guys built the Great Pyramids (which you can see from—ahem—*space*.)

But don't take King Tutankhamun's word for it. In this book, you'll find cold, hard evidence that cats—yes, even the one purring on your lap—might just be a little bit extra (terrestrial, that is).

**Live long and pawspur,
Professor Furnando
Mewton, PhD**

GALACTIC GYMNASTICS

THEY SAY, "CATS ALWAYS LAND ON their feet." As you'll witness, as a cat falls, its slender, flexible body twists and contorts, turning, somersaulting, and floating as it speeds back toward Earth. It's almost as if they're built for zero gravity. Spoiler alert: They are!

According to the philosophy of Occam's razor, the simplest

solution is most often correct.
The simplest solution to why cats
land on their feet? They're aliens,
honing their mid-air maneuvers
for millennia in the zero-gravity
environment of deep space.
Easy-peasy. So, the next time you
marvel at a cat's awe-inspiring
landing prowess, remember. . .
It's not just Earthly instinct; it's a
legacy from the stars.

HIGHER BEINGS

—

SPEAKING OF GALACTIC GYMNAS-
tics, ever caught your cat high
above your head—perhaps atop
the fridge, the mantel, or skillfully
balancing on the narrow edge
of your nose? It's not simply to
look down upon their earthly
subjects or to make you question
the placement of MooMaw's
urn. Maybe—just *maybe*—these
high-flying felines are actually

trying to get a smidgen closer to their interstellar origins. By taking these lofty positions, cats are angling for the best seat in the house to gaze upon their celestial family. Perhaps they're even hoping to intercept an alien cat call from their distant relatives. So, the next time your cat's up high, instead of a scolding, offer a salute to the great beyond— because somewhere out there, a space-cat might just be saluting back.

GROUND CONTROL TO MAJOR TOM(CAT)

HUMANS, IN THEIR INFINITE
naivety, believe they've adopted
cats. LOL! (I'd actually laugh
out loud, but my cat's currently
staring me down, probably
plotting the next phase of world
domination.) The reality? Cats
choose us, and they have their
own nefarious reasons. You see,
these fur-covered extraterrestrials

have been mastering the art of mind control for eons. Every time Señor Fluffykins or Hisston Churchill delicately parks themselves on our laps, they aren't just seeking warmth or comfort. Nope! They are, in fact, activating their mind-control powers. Those deep purrs? Hypnotic frequencies. Those entrancing eye blinks? Subliminal messages. These telepathic "talks" ensure we're perpetually on standby, ready to serve up gourmet kitty chow or embark on

relentless quests to locate that very specific—and very noisy—toy they lost behind drywall last Tuesday. But, remember: resistance is futile. You're already under their spell and, honestly, it's not the worst way to be conquered.

POWER
OF THE PURR

—

THEY SAY, "CATS HAVE NINE LIVES."
And this near-immortality might just
be extended to humans too. Medical
science, ever in its infant stage when
it comes to the alien cats, suggests
that the frequency of a cat's purr
can promote healing in bones. But I
urge you, my fellow Earth-dwelling,
possibly brainwashed by felines,
compatriots, to think beyond the

realms of mere biology. Could it
be that this therapeutic purr, this
rhythmic lullaby that reverberates
deep within our souls, is more
than just nature? Is it, in fact,
evidence of advanced alien tech?

Consider this: our space-savvy kitties, in their boundless cosmic intellect, introduced "purr therapy" to this pale blue dot we call home. Their aim? Healing not just the tangible—our fractured bones, cat scratches (ironically), and the like—but also mending the intangible. The scars on our souls, the shadows in our hearts, and those gloomy Monday blues. I mean, really, who needs a trip to the spa when you've got an intergalactic healer on your lap?

FAR-OUT FELINES

—

EVER NOTICE, WHEN YOU WHIP OUT that trusty laser pointer or flashlight, your feline companion springs to life, chasing the fleeting dot as if their next meal depended on it? In reality, it's probably not hunger driving them. For our feline friends, every beam of light is a reminder of their radiant cosmic origins. Each shimmer echoes the sheen of interstellar comets. Each flash

resembles the glow of distant galaxies. In their eyes, perhaps, these lights are as captivating as E.T.'s glowing finger beckoning them to "phone home."

COSMIC ZOOMIES

SPEAKING OF OTHERWORLDLY wonders, have you ever been lounging on your couch, when out of the blue, your serene kitty transforms into a fur-missile, darting across the room with such ferocity that you fear for your décor (and your ankles)? These sudden, inexplicable bursts of feline energy, lovingly dubbed "the zoomies," always make for quite the spectacle. But

what if, instead of a random burst of kitty energy, the zoomies are really . . . training sessions? Back in their home galaxy, these feline star-travelers engaged in high-speed pursuits, chasing or being chased by cosmic entities. Those unpredictable dashes around your living room? They're keeping their interstellar navigation skills sharp and their reflexes even sharper, readying for the next grand space adventure—or simply evading the vacuum cleaner.

GALACTIC GETAWAYS

—

ANOTHER SCENARIO EVERY CAT
parent knows all too well?
One moment, ye ol' William
Shakespaw is lounging on the
windowsill, echoing Hamlet as he
ponders, "To sleep, perchance to
dream." Then, just as you're about
to serve up that gourmet kitty
dinner . . . poof! She's vanished.
So, what's the deal? Could it be

that these feline magicians are sneaking off for quick jaunts to their home galaxies via cosmic wormholes? Just a brief weekend retreat to their extraterrestrial timeshare, or perhaps a committee meeting on the interstellar best ways to knock over fragile Earth items (re: MeeMaw's urn). Either way, when it comes to these sudden disappearances, the wormhole theory seems as plausible as any.

CAT'S EYE
IN THE SKY

—

SPEAKING OF SPACE TRAVELS AND cosmic adventures, let's talk about those eyes—the deep, mesmerizing eyes of your resident furball. When you really look into them, there's an intensity, an ancient Egyptian wisdom. They're not merely eyes; they're portals to realms beyond our understanding. Ever caught your cat in one of

those intense, far-off stares? It's
not just a vacant daze or a sign
they're plotting their next playful

ambush on your unsuspecting socks. Oh no, it's far grander than that. They're likely revisiting faraway galaxies or perhaps communicating telepathically with their alien counterparts.

Imagine for a moment: Those eyes have witnessed cosmic wonders we can't even begin to fathom. Nebulas being born, stars dying, and E.T. cycling across the moon. (Alright, maybe not that last one, but who knows with these secretive space-cats?)

STARRY
PAW-NDERINGS

—

AS YOU CURL UP TONIGHT, YOUR feline friend purring beside (or, more likely, atop) you, remember to cherish every moment. Whether they're celestial beings from far-flung galaxies or simply the rulers of our hearts and homes, our cats transcend time and space. So, gaze deep into those feline eyes once more, embrace the mysteries

they hold, and continue to ponder the question: Is your cat an alien? Whatever the answer (The answer is yes, BTW), the journey of wonder they take us on is truly out of this world.